The Gospel of Wildflowers and Weeds

Mary Burritt
Christiansen
Poetry Series

Mary Burritt Christiansen Poetry Series
Hilda Raz, Series Editor

The Mary Burritt Christiansen Poetry Series publishes
two to four books a year that engage and give voice to the
realities of living, working, and experiencing the West
and the Border as places and as metaphors. The purpose
of the series is to expand access to, and the audience for,
quality poetry, both single volumes and anthologies, that
can be used for general reading as well as in classrooms.

Also available in the Mary Burritt Christiansen Poetry Series:

*Reflections through the Convex Mirror of Time / Reflexiones tras el Espejo
Convexo del Tiempo: Poems in Remembrance of the Spanish Civil War /
Poemas en Recuerdo de la Guerra Civil Española* by E. A. Mares
The Loneliest Girl: Poems by Kate Gale
Walking Uphill at Noon: Poems by Jon Kelly Yenser
origin story: poems by Gary Jackson
Nowhere: Poems by Katie Schmid
Ancestral Demon of a Grieving Bride: Poems by Sy Hoahwah
The Definition of Empty: Poems by Bill O'Neill
Feel Puma: Poems by Ray Gonzalez
Grief Land: Poems by Carrie Shipers
The Shadowgraph: Poems by James Cihlar

For additional titles in the Mary Burritt Christiansen Poetry Series,
please visit unmpress.com.

THE GOSPEL OF

Wildflowers & Weeds

poems

ORLANDO
RICARDO
MENES

UNIVERSITY OF NEW MEXICO PRESS | ALBUQUERQUE

ISBN 978-0-8263-6399-2 (paper)
ISBN 978-0-8263-6400-5 (electronic)

Library of Congress Control Number: 2022937731

Founded in 1889, the University of New Mexico sits on the traditional
homelands of the Pueblo of Sandia. The original peoples of New Mexico—
Pueblo, Navajo, and Apache—since time immemorial have deep connections
to the land and have made significant contributions to the broader community
statewide. We honor the land itself and those who remain stewards of this land
throughout the generations and also acknowledge our committed relationship
to Indigenous peoples. We gratefully recognize our history.

Cover illustration: courtesy of Social Cut on Unsplash
Designed by Felicia Cedillos
Composed in Adobe Caslon Pro 11/14.5

Contents

I

Ode

The three of us born in Lima, a desert wedged
Between the Pacific & the Andes, it was in Miami
That my siblings & I saw our first rainfall,
A morning downpour so hard, so quick
That parrots bolted from the mahogany trees
& we flapped our arms as each bead splat on sunburnt skin.
How soft & lukewarm sky's waters can be,
Like those motherly teas—linden & chamomile—
Our Cuban Mamá steeped in scoured pots
& left to brood on the stove for all our maladies.
O *lluvia* that soaked our hair, eyes, ears (we almost drowned),
Yet how sweet it was, like iron rust—peppery,
Prune-like on our tongues—& earthier than mold
On the bread Mamá abandoned in cupboards—
Lluvia that formed creeks, puddles & bogs in the backyard
Of mangoes & sausage trees & we (her sacred brood,
She'd call us, her holy kits, cubs, whelps, tadpoles, too)
Played in *el fango*—the mud, the mire, the muck—
Wearing just Fruit of the Loom briefs, tees & cowboy boots
(Even the girl) as we rolled, jumped, slid *a lo loco*,
Moon crazy, clutching clods, catching seeds & grasshoppers
In our first deluge—*aguacero tropical*—& then Mamá
Yelled to keep frolicking, mucking, spitting out rainwater
Like dolphins through their blowholes, these creatures
Of God so blessed to have been born free of sin.

The Blackberry Tree

We had bananas that bore no fruit, an old macaw
stooped on a weathered cross, and a blackberry tree
that grew next to a wall crowned with broken bottles.
The Andes foothills crumbled on a gravel path;
the desert sun broke through the cloak of winter.
I must have been eight or nine when I climbed that tree
to its highest branch and saw over the jags of glass
a bare woman bathing in a brown field, her quick hands
splashing water from an oil barrel, rubbing hard
with a brick of laundry soap until skin glistened
to that newborn bronze before the ravages of patina.
She did not sing but whistled a tune like a reed,
as if puna winds were grazing ichu grass to sighs
of rosary. A toddler ran to her, and she heaved
the crying child to her waist then walked, still wet,
to a zinc hut by a corn patch burnt to stubbled ash.
I climbed down fast and almost sprained my ankle.
At Mass in the Church of the Nazarenes
I had seen women feed their bundled babies
with breasts exposed, and Mamá would pull my lobe,
telling me to think of Mary nursing Baby Jesus
with a shawl of bristly wool as modesty demands.
Our priests taught that flesh is the parchment
of sin and God's suckling grace can be lost
by the smallest transgressions in this world
where goodness fails to root against the weed.
Fifty years on I now know that His Law slants
to love, and I will not eat their bread of shame
leavened with fear. On that blackberry tree
my eyes saw divine beauty: simple, coarse, naked—
this gift of light lifting the fog of humanness.

Altar Boy

after Arturo Rodríguez's 1998 painting Sin Título

I am the altar boy with feet flattened by the catechist's paddle, my
skin toasted like stalks of sugarcane at Lent, my shorts baptized
in the salt pans of saints. I don't wear a mask (God hates carnival)
but a wool hood, Holy Week's, that Sister Rose knitted by the
charcoal altar, her wooden teeth clacking as she hymned in Latin,
the moles on her jowl like prickly pears for penance. My own teeth
are those grates that grilled the martyrs & my little lamb's ears
quiver each afternoon when the wind coughs in fits & pale skies
smoke with incense from a clandestine Mass, perhaps on a runaway
shallop with sails sewn from stolen cassocks, perhaps on a newborn
isle with a thatched church, novices crawling like iguanas around
stations of the cross. There's no home for orphans like us raised in
a convent by the wharf where the footless angel blows his trumpet
for vesper & the abbess marches us to the clapboard altar when the
cock crows. We sleep in straw cubbies, our sheets those crinkled
newspapers that swaddled us like groupers in the foundling's
basket. Hey, you, girl with the twisted neck, your dollhouse will
keep on shrinking between your dirty legs. Not even holy water can
make you clean. Hey, boy, the more you pull on the kite, the more
your house of dreams will get lost in summer's wayward clouds. Let
us live in the meadow, our true home, every bush a hearth, every
pond a font: O blessed loam of nettles whose fireflies light the
shrine at night, whose blue brooks spread out like veins of Calvary.

Ezan

Church of Saint Anthony of Padua, Beyoğlu, Istanbul

Votive lights glow in a pool of wax,
the slim candles upright
on a bed of sand—the eastern way—
no metal racks to stack them
in glass prisons, and thus free to breathe
the myrrh of this Catholic church
across the Golden Horn. I kneel
in front of the crucified Christ,
the boards beneath me wobbly,
worn out, like wood from a shipwreck,
and I must stay steady or crash
into the stone floor and bare to all
my incompetence. I say the Lord's Prayer,
scrambling Spanish and English,
the words broken, stuttered,
finagled, and orphaned by disuse—
how fraudulent my faith
without the rootedness of religion.
Then I hear the call to worship (*ezan*)
from the mosque in Cihangir,
the muezzin's voice on loudspeakers
as he sings the holy words (*allahu akhbar . . .*),
and I feel each Arabic phrase
like a wave gurgled to reverence,
calming our whirlpools of doubt—
or the swells that break into flight
with spindrift wings, warbling surf—
this ocean of faith that inundates
a city astride the cross and crescent moon;
but this time I sense the urge

to pray all in Spanish—*casto y castizo*—
as my own mother would whisper
every Sunday el Padrenuestro
in her lace veil, gown of spotless silk;
and my heart trembles when I see
Christ's hands more like flesh than wood,
his wounds coagulant with sacrifice,
his eyes warm in the brackish light.
I leave bowed, battered, broken into faith
like the old, hunched man bent over
as he rolls his prayer rug on İstiklal Street.

The Transverberation of
St. Teresa of Ávila

In Bernini's statue, eros and the sacred
intersect, conjoin, without diffusion,
without corruption, and where they meet,
as in a Venn diagram, revelation resides,
not in stillness, stasis, but transverberation,
a *striking through*, a *piercing of the flesh*
with a Seraph's golden dart, arrow on fire,
no caduceus, no magic here, but an immaculate
phallus, both corporeal and incorporeal,
that impregnates Santa Teresa's heart
with God's love (the angel a mere go-between),
her face transfixed to infinite swoon,
her hands, her feet candescent in stone,
this miracle we call ecstasy, we call rapture,
both a de-flowering and an in-flowering
that transcends time and space, that violates
reason and sense, so all we can think,
all we can we utter is *pain = bliss, bliss = pain*,
this chasm of chiasmus that baffles us
into faith and surrender because words
are born to flux, thus volatile, mutable (perhaps
only numbers belong to God), this tempest
of transverberation enthralling Santa Teresa
so much that even the folds of her habit
flutter to the austere gales of His apocalypse.

Bernini/Caravaggio

Good art has to be moral, the artist's life strict and dignified,
especially in food. Unlike you, a devourer of flesh, I only eat
fruits in season, modest ones like a prune or a runty apricot.
Carnivores are murderers. Even digesting a hard-boiled egg
or a wedge of sheep's cheese will stain one's soul. *My* bread
is the living Host I take at vesper in chapel, while my hammer
and chisel sleep in the tabernacle. Only at dawn when I pray
in my burlap habit can my hands carve marble soft as dough.
God alone can understand how a brute like you could impregnate
vulgar hemp with piety. How I still shiver seeing your shadows
full of grace, your colors somehow immaculate in their intemperate
palettes, your strokes bold and sure as if the Holy Ghost
had guided your criminal hand. Don't be proud of such a gift.
Nature's error, that is all. A she-wolf should have whelped you
in a den of scat, not a Christian woman on a feathered bed.
What would you have done with my sweet child, St. Teresa?
You would have profaned her with chiaroscuros, her face
that of some harlot from your bordello, your brushwork
cruder than a butcher's cleaver hacking a sheep's shank.
I can hear you boasting now, *My art will outlive my infamies.*
But painting is frail and mutable. Only stone can aspire to eternity.

Homage to the Olive

Olea Europa L. Sativa, tame child of the wild oleaster
that Tuscan nuns harvested with goats' hooves,
not at dawn but dead of Lenten night by torches of suet & sulfur
when the moon goes blind & a gourd carillon
clunked spells to protect the groves from paroxysms of hail;
then the nuns would cure those plumpest varietals
—*picuals* & *picudos*, *tondas* & *coratinas*—
in hogsheads of Dead Sea Brine with laurel-leaf scapulars, asperges
    of lye
& once the novenas were done, the novice fruit
would undergo the sacraments of extraction, racking & pressing,
this trinity of toil that ensured a verdigris oil
blessed with scalding *picantes*, braising *pizzicas*, pluckiest
    pizzicatos—
this holiest of fats they kept in tufa-rock catacombs
safe from venial bitterness or, worse, the heresy of rancidness
& thus the oil preserved its inscape of greenness,
that ooze of God's grandeur gathered & crushed to greatness
by the moonlight of mendicant islands, a grace
that Hopkins could see & smell with his prayerful empathy, his
    ripeness
of patience, his brined humility—O blessed Gerard,
poet of the bruised-bone night who measured joy by jabs of guilt,
who quilted sonnets from sack cloth & Jerusalem thorn,
who was touched by the Holy Ghost in the mauve sunrays
of a Good Friday morning & saw Our Lord of Sorrows
nailed on the olive-wood planks who did not bleed, sweat, or wail
but whose hands, feet & brow wept a fragrant oliveness
& you knelt on the stony ground to savor those trails
of shiny, beaded greenness that foretell Resurrection.

St. Teresa of Ávila upon Reading the *Song of Songs*

I am the sandbur of Sharon & the spurge of Galilee. Crabgrass multiplies under my feet, the bee orchid stings at my touch. I spread the gospel of wildflowers & weeds in the cities & the hamlets, the asylums & the cloisters, the pigsties & the gardens. I suckle the milk thistle as the Angelus tolls to a storm, braise the burdock to eat at the twilight of my beloved's resurrection. A cluster of corn cockles is he to my lips, a bouquet of pimpernels between my breasts, a satchel of bluebells between my legs. O, my Yeshu, you've been gone for days & days, centuries to me. Why do you forsake me? Am I too rude? Too *atrevida*? How I long for you as the buttercup to spring rain. I will find you in the brambles, chase you into the nettles, embrace you among the dandelions. O Nazarene of the fennel forelocks, the blackberry eyes, I will make our bed in the dark earth, digging with my own hands, no lazy shovel or wicked spade, weaving our bed from purslane & wild cotton. You are mine, only mine, to the end of time. Be jealous of me, you daughters of Zion & take this to heart: to woo our Lord you must be stubborn as the fig seed that breaks the rock.

II

Hüzün

after Orhan Pamuk's masterwork, Istanbul

Unlike the Portuguese *saudade* or Italian *mestizia,*
hüzün means more than just melancholy—
rather a communal trauma rooted in the past,
a chronic longing every *istanbullu* feels
for that golden age when Turks ruled continents
and clouds of empire rained down emeralds
on this city where history hazes the air, taints water,
bleeds into stone, and I too can hear the ghosts
of galleasses on the Bosphorus as I roam streets
with cobbles like broken teeth and castaway houses—
rain-wracked, sleet-slashed since Ottoman days.
Raised in Lima until age ten, I too knew
winter's *hüzün* when at the start of May
the sun forsook the city and *limeños* would grieve
the loss of its steadfast light to the cold *garúa,*
ocean mist that smothered the sky with macules
of diesel fume, ash, salty soot. Lima la Triste,
she was called, so sad her spigots wept tears
of tin and the scruffy buzzards drooped on the steel sills
where laundry took days to dry, and Mamá
had to redeem my father's business shirts
with a hot iron and blessings of potato starch.
How we often came down with *catarros*
that made us cough and shiver beneath blankets
prone to mildew, flooding our lungs with phlegm,
and Mamá would succor us with sponge baths
of grain alcohol, warm unctions of VapoRub.

First Communion

Bells barrage, candles quiver, a garrison
of cherubs swarms for revelation's reveille,
and I stand at attention in single file,
hungry for my first chance to ingest the Host
and let it go down in slugs of martial piety.
I clutch a white lily to smite temptation.
A mess jacket, called *esmoquin*, is my flak (vest)
of faith alongside a large armband that hails
the silver chalice as the mortar of Christ's creed.
We march in squads to censorious censers,
squeezing marble missals whose prayers
sputter like buckshot against carnal sin,
and the priest commands us to be manly,
battle-prone, tough as the saints who eat
locusts, drink vinegar of bruised grapes.
Soon Christ's body will transform inside us,
he says, from dough to bone, wheat to marrow,
and we will walk the gauntlets of Our Lord.
We kneel at the smoky altar with purpled knees,
jellied eyes, jaws quick to clench like vises,
though my own tongue feels the warm wafer
as something feminine, soft, tickly—a feather
of flour—not hard and coal-hot as I had feared
in catechism when boys would prick thumbs
with thorns like St. Rose and St. Martin of Porres.
But on this day of sacrament I divine that the body
is not sinful but the vessel of human goodness,
where God's love pulses in every limb, organ, cell—
how pleasure is the blessed conduit of His grace.

Grace

We cannot buy it in bulk at Trader Joe's,
Swap it for gold, or hoard shares of Grace, Inc.,
To hedge against bad luck. We acquire it
Without contract, promissory notes, or IOUs,
Neither codicils nor fine print. We gather
Grace safe from litigation or severance,
And though we might breach the strictures of creed,
It cannot be forfeited or suspended. Rather,
Grace is asymmetric, parabolic, skewed to love,
Immanent and absolute, but also unpredictable
As quantum particles, both here *and* there,
Both full *and* empty, so it might arrive
Inopportunely and thus slip under hope,
Upsetting the earnest prayer, teasing our faith,
Like some rain bands, copious cumuli,
That appear astray, unbidden, in stagnant skies
To drench at last the drought-scourged earth.

Triptych Number 1: Fidelio Ponce

I. He Comes Around at Vesper Time

after Ponce's undated painting Novices

The Brides of the Lamb are growing old
in their convent of coconut fronds with coral-rock floors;
the gulls awaken them at first light each day
to pray with porcelain hands, soot-veined, salt-scabbed;
their spines, fragile as quills, skew to benediction
as they trod to a shrine inside a tree hollow,
their small heads drooping from leaden scapulars.
They envy Christ, who remains young
with lacquered hair and jasmine cerements.
He comes around at vesper time to eat guavas and smoke
a maduro cigar beneath his canopy of palms,
and though they take great pains to massage his feet
in aguardiente, bake those sugary confections
of egg yolk they learned from the Carmelite nuns,
Christ glances at them sideways, without a word or any touch.
But they do not fuss or grouse about their plight.
Their spouse is just plain tired of being divine,
they believe, so often jabbering away about his cousin John
kissing him in the river or those spring mornings
when he and Judas tossed the lambs of Bethlehem.
The past cannot be changed, and youth is a chimera
of deceit, so the Brides take solace in knowing
that marriage means having knees knotted as mahogany
and that the sweat of their brows is the vinegar
of salvation. Pure they live and pure they will die
in their bamboo cells as they count the days
with bread crumbs, and every Sunday they will wash

their sins away with lye soap of the gospel.
And when is their day of joy, their time of glory?
Easter Sunday when their husband returns
from Golgotha with passionflowers, quince angels,
and custards beatified with the darkest rum.

II. Manifesto

In that studio by the sea, a shack full of black pigeons and cannibal
crabs, I sought my muse in hunger and thirst, drinking the baptismal
turpentine, eating the lead of Cremnitz white that is the skin of Jesus
in the womb, tasting the linseed oil that christens a canvas on its
easel of fear. My gift is to deny the tropics, deny joy, deny the sensual.
I am El Greco born in Camagüey, where the churches are humble,
the trees ashen, and even the cows graze on the bitter grass of Lent.
I wish I'd been born in a faraway land of snow and ice where the
sun hides behind tungsten clouds, not like in Cuba where sunlight
is vulgar, those lascivious hues that corrupt one's faith. I am truer
to Christ's creed than he ever was. My mission is to smother Eden
with bladder greens, dun blues, muddy ochers. My palette is faithful
to the simplicity of martyrdom, pure as the withered lungs that will
take me to the paradise of the poor. So what if I get drunk on hand-
me-down booze and wander the city in linen rags. So what if I mix
my whites with too much oil, let the paste crack and creak on my
canvases, let my spatula unload all my grievances against the rich,
against the prissy painters, against the priests who speak with two
tongues. Pure white, acrid and acrimonious, is the color of heaven,
the color of spectral saints, the color of my own tubercular blood as it
worms its way to resurrection.

III. The Brines of Good Friday

after Ponce's circa 1944 painting The Procession

Despite how hard they might pray
Kneeling on gravelly corn,
Children learn from priests and mothers
That the sun will betray their joy
On Easter day and boil their fleecy clouds
To muddled sobs of lanolin rain—
How their little boats of wax
Will set sail from coral shrines
Yet find no haven from the melting sun
In the still waters of Galilee.
The saints say that to resist fate
Is pride that must be snuffed out
Like silt packed into a blenny's gills,
This tiny Galilean fish that knows
Its place in the great chain of being
And will not pretend it's a barracuda
Or a requiem shark destined for heaven—
Just as God's children must forfeit
Their earthen innocence and be reborn
As gill-breathing acolytes who will swim
The brines of Good Friday in high-
Tide processionals, hoisting keeled crosses
That cut the waves into wakes of revelation.
How their mothers will follow them
In whale-bone canoes, these women
Of crimson clay who serve their Lord
Without food, water, or even sweet air
As they paddle astride their young,
Who have learned that agony is liquor
That titillates on Passion days.

Requeté, Soldier of God

Battle of the Ebro, Spanish Civil War, 1938

Our standard is a crucifix, our battle cry "Long Live Christ the King!", our rifles blessed with the milky snow of Our Lady of Montjuich, who watches over us with eyes of ice as we march to Ave Marias against the cold wind. She speaks to me in credos of mortar and doxologies of artillery. *Slay all the reds who spread the plague of bolshevism on our holy land.* I vow to you, Mary of the Mountain, that our España will bear again the yoke of love, the hymnal rack, the gridiron of the Eucharist. Let the thuribles of gunpowder sway at Mass. Let the Inquisition pummel the faith like a storm on a fallow field. I am the Exterminating Angel, pure of heart, pure of mind, my belt the scourge of His Passion, my beret the color of His blood. Zealotry is the snow that falls on Our Lady's Peak, every crag a nipple of her breast, every stone a teardrop of her joy. Beware the idle mind, she warns. Be suspicious of pretty words from ugly mouths. Rote prayers clean the mind of sin. No fancy thoughts. Only a thinker's pen will stray into heresy or, worse, Russian ungodliness. I am a simple man of faith. When I fire bullets I spread the seeds of Our Lord, each one sprouting a crown of thorns. Behold how the grenade when tossed by a pious hand becomes the pomegranate of Easter, exploding with splinters of Calvary, steel hymnals, leaden beads.

St. Apollonia, Patroness of Dentists

On Judgment Day the righteous will rise from their graves with milk
teeth immune to caries, rosy gums that never canker. No one will
have to wear braces, caps, crowns, or bridges, even those horseshoe
contraptions that teeth grinders wear in their sleep. Glorious will
be the end-time of the alveoli, the revelations of dentine. In the
meantime, as we await the end of pyorrhea, tartar & gingivitis,
spread my gospel of dental hygiene to all the continents, to every
island, across all isthmuses. Teach the unclean to floss as they pray, to
wash their mouths with vinegar, to soak their choppers in limewater.
Indulge those converts who brush five times a day with dentifrice of
bitterweed, no lazy electric brushes, no namby-pamby nylon bristles,
only hedgehog quills. Exalt the most pious who bear their mouths
at the confessional of drill, probe & pincer, jubilant to have an
incisor pulled, a molar ground, or a cavity filled with brimstone, their
faith hard, raw, pure as they spurn psalms of antiseptic, novenas of
Novocain, loathsome heresies in the eyes of Our Lord.

Tower of Babel

Praise be to God for confounding our tongues and scattering us into exile
like chaff in a stray wind or the fig seeds dropped by a green *iguaca*
on a hog plum. Confusion is sweetest chirimoya on a dry tongue.
Hymns of disorder bring bountiful harvests in times of drought,
and perhaps only cross-eyes can see in chaos serene mandalas.
I shout from the top of my Babel's tower sown as a kapok tree—
Blessed are the dialects, the patois, the argots, and the pidgins;
the half-breed word-hoards and the mongrel grammars; the Geechees,
the *calós*, and the ghost words; those hallowed languages gone dead
or, worse, extinct because of genocide or conquest or just time's erosion,
yet how we must mourn each one in our bones, hearts, spleens;
then join hands by the sea at dawn to chant their names in flames
of gumbo-limbo, O so many to remember: Elmolo, Mawa, Ba-Shu,
Koibal, Guanche, Calusa, Wichita, and the Taíno of my own island—
Kubanakán—whose words linger past the cyclones of our sadness
like flotsam chromosomes or castaway fossils of such beautiful amber
as *barbacoa, canoa, fotuto, hamaca, iguana, malanga, tabaco, yuca*.
With these words I make machines of memory in flesh and marrow.
With these words I glide and cleave the tidal waves of history.
With these words I take root in the quicksands of diaspora.

The Sacrifice of Isaac

You feared God more than you loved your son.
Obey, obey, obey, the fire angels tolled in song:
The covenant demands Isaac's blood be shed
On Mt. Moriah. *Heap stones into an altar*, so said
Adonai. *Make a crib of sticks and consume to ash*
Your only son. You sacrificed reason: *A rash*
Heart is a perfect heart. To flinch, to question,
To hesitate at all would have caused you to *sin*
Against God, and thus your hand clamped Isaac's neck,
Your *shochet*'s knife steadfast to make the nick
That would spill the blood of the boy who asked,
"But where is the lamb?" You lied for the task,
Old man, your will unbent by Isaac's shouts.
Where was your fatherly grace to defy such slaughterhouse
Of faith? Though the angel did halt you in time
(Ram in the bush), you meant to carry out the crime
Against Isaac since duty breaks bonds of blood
And all affection splinters to kindle, altar's wood.

Would I have done the same, my son, Adrian,
The paschal lamb? To say *no* would bring the ban—
Herem—to eat mud, to drink brine, to roam
Alone in coal-tar skies, fields of spiked bone.
To save my boy I'd trample on duty, rip apart
The covenant. Let my soul become a dust cart,
My skin sackcloth. I'd breathe, like salt air, *pariah.*
I'd own the butcher's blade. Love, not the law,
Will be my prayer. The human, not the divine—
This ragged, restless world my only shrine.

Théophile Gautier in Istanbul

*As I have already said, it is my habit, in strange towns,
to plunge boldly into unknown streets, like a nautical explorer; trusting to the
points of the compass and dead-reckoning.*

—*Théophile Gautier*, Constantinople of To-Day, *1854*

O city of felines rubbing against my leg in the porticos of squamous light,
my city of filaments in the air that flap into swallows of desire,
my city of veiled Philomels with small feet & long graceful arms &
    green eyes
that glow between the rocks & the weeds. At every naked corner

I feel the glare of your candles on the weathered sills & they speak to
    me too,
chattering, *Come inside, flat-footed man, and die on this bed of stone.*
This truth I know: There's mildew in every dream of joy. And a sober life
is sure to shoo away the Muse. From lane to lane, from square to square,

I hear the hobbled men hawking mussels in broken shells & women
    smashing stumps
of dough on griddles like a camel's hump. I see their glares,
their frowns, their bitten lips. Do they loathe me as much as oil hates
    vinegar?
Or maybe it's just fear when those snickering boys stomp on my boots,

asking, *Who are you that rambles in the night, a ghost, a raven man?* I will
    find salvation
in your fallen city. Watch me suckle your mulberry runts,
watch me bless the dawn, watch me charm your sea into whirlpools of
    grace.
I will not desist in finding God, mine & yours, on these alleys & cul-de-
    sacs—

way, way beyond the city walls where I will touch, smell, kiss the
wings of God
the Man, God the Woman, God the Child & the cypress will grow
feathers in spring & just my touch will make the old wooden houses
go back to being trees
& between stone walls a moldy seed will burst into an evergreen of
you & me.

Dalí at Port Lligat, 1936

Federico is dead, the duende said in a dream of blue mastic
by a turpentine sea, and Dalí howls to the tide, sobbing
spindrift, his bunioned feet kneading the sinking sand
like a purring cat, and he regrets to have never kissed
Fede's mouth, sloppy as a pomegranate bursting at carnaval.
He had almost whispered *te adoro* into that soft-shell ear
of versicles, fondled his groin as a boy might grapple a hagfish,
but shame made him stop in that twilight of summer
when anchovies fry to ecstasy in cauldrons of olive oil.
                         As always, Dalí seeks sanity in art,
but Fede's death causes him a phobia of pigments and graphite.
He cannot paint anymore or look at a painting without retching—
sulks barefoot in the sand, quaffs flagons of fish blood to numb the pain.
Grief is deceitful, he thinks, and loving a man is a nightmare
of locusts nibbling your skin like camembert. To love a woman
without sex is the cure, he realizes, and Gala as wife will be his muse,
model, and mentalist. How each morning with a boy's delirium
he'd conduct stoic Gala to his studio and repaint stale eyes
to Venus flytraps, butter buttocks with soft Italian umber,
tweak her dun mouth to a sea urchin prickling with desire.

Mercato del Pesce, Catania

Sacks of snails to pluck, capuchin cuttlefish to martyr in a pan
& serve with parsley wreaths, lemons mildewed to patina.
Girls gut mullet for roe; cats in cortege mewl the mackerel man.
Sunlight steeps the octopi, gleaming purple as ice begins to thaw
& the mongers call out to stilettoed signoras in baritones of opera,

Monkfish to stew with capers, she-crabs to boil for your love.
But clouds pour a salty rain & the terraces of fish begin to melt
in a landslide of blood, scales & gills that draws a dark drove
of urchin botflies, bat-winged worms from Mount Aetna that pelt
signoras with pestilence; they cry out to God but trip in the salt-

slushed cobblestones, their heels weaponized to slice silicone
accoutrements to calamari & the mangled matrons bellow
like St. John's trombones to be heard as far as Papal Rome,
the mongers too wailing how their big sardines will have to go
for cat food in Tripoli, but just off the boat the tuna men show

off their hordes of albacore, bluefin, bigeye to butcher for the grill,
those copper pans of bouillabaisse, the sushi bars of Singapore.
The mongers chant shanties to fishy St. Peter, sure that a miracle
had saved them from salt's apocalypse when the sea will go to war
with humans & the fish, crabs, octopi settle their ancient score.

Off-Off-Variation on Théophile Gautier's "Promenade Nocturne"

As the mermaid girls dance on the lichenous rocks,
The moon-maimed men howl for love on Galata Bridge.
Old anglers toss them sardines, beat pails to song,
But the men howl louder still to the mermaid girls,
Give us love, or we'll drown in the Marmara Sea.
Agate-scaled & lamprey-lipped, the *deniz kizlari* hear
Their plight among the seagull screaks & onward
They swim to meet their destiny in waters deep
& dark where they were spawned twenty years before
When the tides defied the will of the moon & sleet
Of verdigris fell on Istanbul. The men see their bodies
Sparkling in moonlight & so they wait on all fours,
Yelping sweet-nothings, slobbering in glee, certain that
Their love would be returned. But the *deniz kizlari*
Have another plan: consumption, degustation, that urge
To feed on men, cannibal's aliment (what is digestion
But a godly joy) & soon they ride those supple backs,
Hissing spindrift spells, puffing their gills to incite
The moon-maimed men who soon comply like husbands
Henpecked in their bridal pens, such carnivorous striptease
For all to see & hear—the fish, the fishers, the sailors
Startled on their skiffs—this frenzy of hungry love
Like a litter of angels sucking hard on teats of nebulae—
Hurry, hurry, *deniz kizlari* & slurp those last drops
In night's canopy of cockled stars & bladdery clouds.

St. Lapsia, Patroness for
Catholics Lapsed & Re-Lapsed

Bored with Santiago & Fatima on those lazy days
of Lent? Does the psychedelia of Hieronymus Bosch
entice you? Come stroll in St. Lapsia's garden
by a violet shore where wrought-iron willows give shade
to ponds of liquid lead & red-beryl cherubim dive
for chrysocolla crabs. Feed blue poppies to pink sheep
in the purple pastures of Galilee. Hike her fields
where the cacti of Christ prickle novices to giddiness,
then join her acolytes—pubescents all in Gloria Dei—
to shoot scree of votive glass, chip stones to sacred hearts.
Your destiny, your joie de vivre? St. Lapsia agrees
that simple play is a sacrament. Let adulthood wilt away
& dance the fandango when her toadstones of rain
drum the earth to mammee-apple song. St. Lapsia looks on
from the campanile of her convent on Naseberry Hill,
so make her your confidant, your mediatrix, this first-
born of sibyls among all Hieronymites, bon vivant
of penitents, dead-raiser, tongue-twister, whose hands
grow stigmatic orchids every spring, the most incorruptible
of saints with BO of jasmine & frangipani warts.
St. Lapsia will give you an apotheosis of sugar & molasses,
every cloud a coconut bonbon to give you warmth
in Christ's Troposphere & you will rocket piggyback
to his throne on the pinnacle of a baobab bigger
than a ziggurat & be his beloved for a minute or two
(but don't grouse—aren't you luckier than those spinsters,
male or female or both, who whittle crosses all day?)
& you will take your sweet time smooching chirimoya lips,
tweaking cashew lobes, teasing mahogany locks
& know at last, at last the love of the man called God.

Sister Aurea, OCD, Rails against the Animals to Her Third Graders

To loathe the animals is our sacred calling, far and above chastity and
obedience. Shame on St. Francis for coddling the beasts, all of them
capricious, selfish, dirty, thus our duty to enforce order and discipline.
Spare the prod, spoil the beast, says the Bible. Who told St. Martin
that doves, cats, and mice would get along, let alone drink milk from
a common bowl? God orders us to tame all brutes of the field, the air,
the sea. To breed them dumb and slow, quick to butcher, sweet to eat.
How about caramel hides, boys and girls, candy-cane bones, cookie-
dough steaks? God's one and only mistake was to create those cute
critters you love to pet, chase, coo in a cage. Write this down in your
prayer books. Songbirds are corpse nesters, poopers with wicked
aim. Gerbils will gnaw our belly buttons as we sleep. Kittens leap
from ledges to bite our ears and noses. When a puppy frolics with
a ball, Satan comes out to bait our souls. Not just the live ones but
toy animals tempt us to sin. Good children must play with stones,
deadwood, iron nails.

St. Tatua, Patroness of Tattooists

I am the daughter of Queequeg & a runaway nun. I doodle gospels
on palms & soles, bead necks with rosaries, tap amulets around the
eyes, my needle a nail from the cross, my ink Christ's blood. Beware
of baptism by water, evaporative & thus prone to deceit. Ink those
babies, Mother says, or else it's Limbo to the end of time. I engrave
nativities on their newborn backs, cut crosses into foreheads, inscribe
calves with my father's chant. *Mehe tua 'oe! Mehe tua 'oe!* You are as
god! You are as god! Mother says tattoos must mark the skin to be
holy. Stick-ons & henna are anathema. In the past my acolytes were
few—sailors, whores, prisoners—but now even the cupcake baker
scores her belly with flaming hearts. By my hand, psalms will snake
around your arms, the beatitudes grace your buttocks, Golgotha's
graffiti arching ocher brows. And at life's end, I'll flay your skin, neck
to foot & bleach it clean, at sunrise, then hang it to dry in Polynesian
winds forty days & nights, my godsent parchment to tattoo hymns
to the fish & the whales on All Soul's Day.

Ave Maria

in memory of Richard Crashaw

Virgin, Virgin full of grace,
Sea Lilies in a crystal vase,
Bless my hands, my feet, my face
    In the spindrift of Lenten seas
At Passiontide; holy is your brume
That soothes wounds, stings, welts (the bloom
Of martyrs who woo the blood moon
    At Calvary) & I, too, will see
Bethlehem's star on that dark night,
Your son born from a seed of light,
God's word made flesh to incite
    Blood-spark, bone-spurt, organ-spree,
This obstinate life in the ocean
Of your womb whose waters christen,
Whose salt absolves all our sins.

St. Lucy, Patroness of
Those Troubled by Their Eyes

after Zurbarán's 1633 painting Santa Lucia

Do not bemoan your myopia, your glaucoma, your astigmatism. Be
grateful for any infirmity, whether the grand macular degeneration
or the pinkeye. Blessed is the child born blind, for vision, as
St. Augustine says, beckons the worst sins: vanity, lust, and
gluttony. How beauty misguides us into pleasure; how daylight
distorts with lavish colors. Embrace night's austerities; spurn the
sun's seduction. In the darkest chapel let your contrite eyes misalign
by the light of naphthalene. Severity will assure they go astray,
bleary, or cross. Why wait until old age endows them with the
wisdom of cataracts? Go ahead, my children, lance those wicked
eyes with cactus needles, pluck out those lids with iron pincers,
singe those brows with Paschal candles. How happy you will be
to smell the world as never before, our holiest sense, so says St.
Augustine. Everything in Heaven smells divine, don't you know?
God's mouth, St. Michael's pee, or the underarm of a martyr. Even
Purgatory is fragrant where penitents' sweat is the frankincense
that lifts a lost soul to the raptures of Paradise.

G_d

Absolutely incorporeal,
Wh_se immanence—Einstein discovered—
Exerts gravitational attractions
Upon substance and thought alike

Wh_se force cannot be measured
By Newtonian physics—
Having no mass and acceleration

Wh_ casts no dice, no cowries,
And conceived numbers before
H_ uttered photon and molecule

Wh_se priests divine
With cometary decimals
And black-hole zeroes—
The infinite values of π and ה

The Nuclear Scientist
Code-Named Ismail Avows Holy War

Blessed is the scientist who can hear God's call in the whirr of a
centrifuge, who can see God's eyes in globes of plutonium, who can
smell God's breath in a mushroom cloud. What is a missile but the
Prophet's sword and radiation the sirocco of his jihad. Sacred are
the quantum laws of my Koran, every formula a hadith, every chain
reaction a call to salah, every shock wave a creed of faith. I will rain
down neutrons on all the infidels, the apostates and the heretics too.
Doesn't violence redeem the wicked, and a nuclear blast vaporize the
soul to grace? My fallout will cleanse the world in a holy hecatomb,
and we men of God will then build from the ruins our caliphate,
where the sun never sets in disgrace. Pity is the bane of piety, and
benevolence a disease. Don't ever break bread with a Jew or let your
clean fingers touch a cross. The mosque is a battlefield where I dream
fireballs that scorch twilight's veil and cense the clouds with gamma
dust, halos' purple light, ionized skies where angels swarm for holy
war. From minarets of molten gas, I hear the call to squeeze the sun.

Atonement

Cartoon from *Deutsche Zeitung Tageblatt*—Nov. 28, 1938—
The Grand Inquisitor shakes the bloodied hand of a Nazi:
Congratulations, dear colleague! You've really far outdone us!!

Eichmann : Torquemada
Edict of Expulsion : Final Solution
Limpieza de Sangre : Aryan eugenics

Why do [we] forget
Ιησούς/Iesus/Jesús
how the mohel's blade
blessed you
on the eighth day?
You of Israelite lineage
going back
to King David
You who were presented
at the Temple
as the law of Moses said

[We] made you wear Treblinka hairshirt
crowned you with barbed wire
starved you with Hosts of sawdust
gassed you with thuribles of Zyklon B
cremated you in death's-head tabernacle
& your fragrant smoke ascended to heaven

On this Holy Day of Teshuvah
{I} steep in the mikveh bath
wear linens of Aaron
light the lamps for the living & the dead
offer incense of Nineveh

Thrice sounding the shofar
{I} sing the tehillah:
O thou that hearest prayer,
All flesh shall come before thee . . .

Forgive [us] King of the Jews
Yeshu ben Yoseph
Dancer-of-the-mysteries
Torah made flesh
Talmudist of silence
Mad lover
Elohim

IV

Hear Me, Hart Crane

It was on a small island in the Gulf of Batabanó
That you built your bridge across the East River,
Cuba's sun the furnace that forged steel cables
From aerial roots of banyan and strangler fig
Innocent of ice fog, hail burst, acid snow.
Your mind smelted our mangrove nurseries,
Slabbed our coral beds, wrenched our cradles
Of epiphyte into cantos of Manifest Destiny.
Outside that cluttered study, caisson of your craft,
Grew an old mango tree trussed with blue liana
Whose vines you plucked to metal iambs
Till such tender wood could not bear the wrack
Of your industrial winch, clamp, crowbar.
I cannot blame you, dear Hart, for don't we all
Make art from paradox? I have lived long
In the monster's entrails, longer than Martí,
To know that twisted fate is more gift than curse—
As I did years ago when I wrote my first book
(Pure Caribe—*magia y manigua*—no apologies)
In that apartment by Chicago's lakeshore,
Gazing out the window each winter morning
To tropicalize snowbanks into coral cays
And melt those slush puddles to swamplands
De la rana, el caimán, la jutía conga, el catey.
The snow pebbles scattered to papaya beads,
And the trestles of icicles swung like garlands
Of Bougainvillea against tall royal palms
I lathed from the blizzard-blighted poles.
And in the cold wind or in those lake flurries
I'd hear our *ruiseñor* trill her cascabel song.

Letter to José Lezama Lima

O apostle of our tropical baroque, so lush your verse,
so snarled, crusted, curdled, mottled & spirally—
it was you who taught me that excess (the more extravagant
the holier) is our island's sacrament & the creed
of spareness just a heresy bound to the northern mind.
Ay Lezama mío, poeta de poetas, I heard your call
in the rummed rivulets of jasmine nights, annona days—
seek out our splurging sun, heed our fecund heat,
soak in the placental rains that bless our Antilles
with a reckless greenness & only then can you see
habaneras as okra-fingered, tamarind-toed, ackee-
eyed, with little guava mouths that froth meringue
when the sun goes down & hummingbirds swarm.
They stroll with *danzón* shimmies those long esplanades
of soursop foam along a coconut bay. They twirl
banana-skin parasols that sieve sunlight into aureoles.
Their little cinnamon dogs chew on marzipan bones.
How absurd, the penny-pinching realist might say,
she who reads poetry like an actuary table
and commands that I be true as a T-square or a compass.
She hates dreams, idylls, curves, the ampersand.
She is the Angel of Order in a world graced by disorder.
She haunts us as judge, inquisitor, reason's enforcer
who demands that all paradoxes be seized at the border
then put into stocks beneath the syllogistic tree—
that every carefree trope be corralled into dungeons
of dogma because the imagination when unrestrained
leads to chaos. I hear you murmur in sea-cadenced agony,

What is reality but the tyrant that torments our art,
the cudgel & lash that beat out whim & reverie?
Blessèd Lezama, I believe in your gospel of the baroque,
the fire of your candle tree when the wind is wet,
the blood of your banana blossom at break of dawn.

Triptych Number 2: Carlos Enríquez

I. Yeguas

in conversation with Enríquez's 1941 painting Landscape with Horses

Sea-borne winds whirl into cochineal skies, unravel a garland
of sweetsop clouds, roar into ramshackle hills
that breed the anopheles & the pearl-eyed boa, thrashing a clutch
of royal palms, tall, slender & wind-whittled
as your own brushes of pig's bristle / weasel's hair, those round, flat &
     bright pinceles
you wield like a bone wand, *palo de brujo*, priest's asperges—
O Carib caduceus that blesses our cyclone-prone island
with embroideries of bush, weed & sprout, filigrees of the epiphyte
& the strangler fig, veneers of mold, moss & mildew.
Ay pintor de la tierra, how well you knew in your cassava bones &
     soursop heart
that to be pure & sovereign our island must be reborn as Kubanakán
when humans brewed prophecies of cohoba, hovered like
     hummingbirds
atop purple canopies, rode the hammerhead shark on a full moon.
I swim your river of green lightning that splits apart the green
     meadows
of foragers & I smell, hear, see a herd of wild horses,
lithe & skinny as the palms behind them, delicate in their stride,
unwary of any swerve of wind, some of the mares among them
drinking from the river, this slow, dense water, molasses of mercury,
that slides down swales of cinnabar muck where I crawl
like a mudfish, roll down the riverbank, swallowing this dough
of clotted earth & as the glowworms burst into flame
I realize these *yeguas* are my brethren, my blood, my very breath—

so then like Adam who named the animals I unchristen them
for all eternity, uttering just neighs & whinnies, spiting the saddle too,
the bit, reins, stirrups & with savage gait I am free to run
alongside for a hundred leagues, days on end, never out of breath
or hampered in stride, stubborn on instinct, our destiny
not a dwelling or a homestead but a horizon of burnt emerald
where the angels of the hurricane tremble the cotton-silk trees.

II. Manifesto

Only in those bucolic landscapes that clutter the Louvre is nature
submissive. Art emasculates wind, water, and wood. The language
of beauty is the language of conquest, and the sublime an ornament
of empire. When I walk in the sun of my island, my skin sweats
to a reptilian scaliness that is natural, uncontrived, unlike velvet or
some animal hide wrought to deceive. The tropics engender disorder
and paradoxes. The straight line does not exist in *la manigua*, where
everything is curves and deviation, where life's colors mix with the
shadows of death. Our rainclouds drop grapeshot, our rivers sunder
stones to chicken bones, and these stones when swept to earth
become seeds of sorcery. I paint our nature blindfolded using just my
senses of smell and touch. *La manigua* dominates me, and I let her.
One has to be an animal to understand her in one's blood, to feel her
in one's marrow, to hear the murmurings of her seas. My brush is a
machete, my canvas the bark of strangler fig, my colors boiled from
weeds, bugs, slugs. The fine painter is an impostor, a spy, a charlatan
in the eyes of the gods of the hurricane and the yuca. The Taínos
knew how to carve stones and shells into sacred vessels. The sound
of the rain was the music of their hearts. We killed them so long
ago in the mines and the bonfires, but they endure in the trees and
the lagoons. I am not of their blood, but I hear them in my dreams.
Don't be timid, they tell me. Be sincere as the scorpion and wise as
the barracuda. Learn from them to forge the art of our island: wild
and unpredictable as a rush of water that heaves the dry loam to
quickening.

III. Elegia

after Enríquez's 1937 painting Charcoal Oven

O men of the cayman's swamp
And the charcoal trees called *marabú*,
This burning mound is your tower
Of Babel on this island of brine dusks
Where the moon confuses the sun,
And the turpentine light of terebinth clouds
Will not peep through with revelation
Because the shekinah of Sinai cannot breathe
In these Antilles too green, too wet
For such a desert god without a name—
So any tropical fire must be profane
As it cooks the flesh of guiltless brush
To *bruto carbón*, dark as night's marrow,
You sell to city folk who haggle you,
Bilk you, trap you with false covenants,
So you find no soul's recompense, no sacrament
Of agape, and what is your sole reward
But threadbare pesos in a flyblown satchel,
Your backs, arms, and chests sun broiled,
Crack-prone as you cram *sacos de carbón*
Onto a flat-bottom boat, your brood
Of black bundles that will huddle together
On a dark night like castaways or refugees
Clamoring for water in a rainless sea.

Turuqueira

Sister Yara, square-jawed, hairless Carmelite
of the Caribbean rule, trods the talcum sands
of Turuqueira to her convent on a coral swale,
singing the rosary in chirps, churrs, and trills—

avian Taíno, tongue of the first martyrs,
who saw Mother Atabey rise from the east
in a canoe of blue fire and trouble the swells
to wreck the Spaniards' ships on Easter Day.

It is early morning, time for the first Mass.
Gusts toll the barnacled bells of sunken galleons.
Conger eels flail from mainmasts crowned
with the jaws of requiem shark, stingray barbs.

Stopping at every twelve yards to sign the cross,
Sister Yara balances a wheelbarrow of infants,
mostly bald boys diapered with jute, their moles
like black beans, lips of ackee, cashew lobes.

"Priests are useless as a sixth toe on a bad foot,"
so she will baptize them herself at sunset
in her chapel of quarried bones, using seawater
and gourd, canticles of conch, as the Taínos

once did on the leeward side of Turuqueira,
with its coconut coves, sweetsop copses,
and soft cacao soils where the ancestors' faith
flourishes free of the rigors of Church and prelate.

In her island Vatican, holy empire of ceiba,
sea grape, and jagüey fig, she will catechize
their mothers—pickers, weavers, water carriers—
to the creed of Mother Earth, Father sky,

sing hosannas to the hurricane and cassava root,
red-papaya benedictions—108 black seeds—
and they will birth more sons of the earth,
twice blessed by the steaming sun, swarming rain,

and their daughters too will become *sirenas*
at twelve years old, sprouting gills, fins, air bladders
to dive into mercuric eddies, swim the littorals
of Mother Atabey, when they will dream

the Paradisum, back to that time when only the sea
had life, and we will then be free to shed
this mammalian guise to return as creatures
of the tidepool, shoal, ría, lagoon, coral reef,

and only then will the requiem shark, O *tiburón*,
be ascendant once again, Selachian Seraphim,
who prays for prey in the atolls of Our Lord—
deepwater hierophant, apostle of blood and brine.

Caliban to the Sea Nymph Ananai

after Theocritus's The Idylls

Not tomorrow, not at neap tide when the dog star dies,
but marry me now as the barracuda spawns
the angels of war and the coconut trees clatter canticles
in a wind-racked shore. O my brackish Ananai,
let us wed among the yearling mangroves when the tide is low
and the muck bubbles like the fat of a roasting sow.
My love for you is feral, indomitable.
I would hurl my spear a mile high, wounding the dawn-lit sky,
just to caress once more your sargassum tresses,
your mako skin, your moon-jelly eyes. Let our bridal canoe—
worm-bored, mussel-gnarled—tear apart the billows
and take us to my leeward island—Alliouagana—
where fire-gilled cherubim frolic among manatees,
and I have domain over the cassava, the hutia, the hurricane.
Let us breed a continent of creatures, neither earth
nor water like you and me but both and thus blessedly impure,
our cosmic whelps that will propagate in the millions
across every island, isthmus, bight, peninsula, mainland,
then cross the Atlantic in caravels of bone, gristle, cured skin
to reconquer Europe, raze every hamlet and city
to be rebuilt as citadels of strangler fig, mazes of maize,
coral coves for the hammerhead and the barracuda,
such joyful revenge against our old masters,
who brought us slavery and plague, plundered our forests
for galleons, battlements, palaces, the crucifix.

The Patriarch Jakob as an Arawak

Born to the Taíno tribe by the grace of Elohim-Yukahu—
                    O Jakob of Ouanalao, gar-scaled,
shark-mouthed patriarch of the Antilles, Ancient of Islands—

Kneel before him as he wrestles the green caiman with whirling spins,
his arms big as banyan boughs, his serrated teeth, all thirty-three,
                    stripping the beast's bellyto be hanged
on holy days by menorahs of tibial bamboo.

      Hear the shamans give Jakob praise every full moon
            when he slays the uncircumcised Caribs who ransack the manioc mounds
& kidnap the mermaids of his village.

                    Bold Cacique, they sing, Wily Breeder of Warriors,
Annihilator of Infidels, so many names it takes hours to recite—

                    Hail Jakob, pious
to a fault, who burns salted tobacco in a shrine of manchineel by the sea,
      snorts datura for visions of the fire clouds that come before the hurricane,

but he's proud too—magnificent bragger—who swears he's the strongest
                    nabori on earth,beating his chest, huffing smoke,
wiggling his buttocks of manatee, shouting to the heavens:

I can pin down anyone, anything, even you, my creator in the clouds—

Elohim-Yukahu, a god prone to anger, quick to punish, sends his champion Uriel
            to slam down Jakob as he sleeps in his hammock,

& Uriel (cannibal of cherubs, crocodilian hierophant, with three flaming heads,
        sucker hands, armored tail)

throws down Jakob on the red earth, wrestling till daybreak, a flurry of lifts,
        trips, slams, overhooks, tie-ups, near falls,

& Jakob the tamer of caimans prevails against the angel, but not before Uriel
      bites into his right leg, deep into the marrow, leaving behind an iron fang,
which leaves Jakob limp, wobbly footed, a cane walker for the rest of his life,

but it's no curse for him, more a gift for shamans to sing about, record in petroglyphs—
      O Jakob the blessed one who pokes his wound
& feels the pain of prophecy, where to find the tree of life with its fruit of flesh,

      where to find the sinkholes of sweet water in times of drought,
his final warning in a daydream to fight the smelly, bearded men who will
      soon come from beyond the sun on canoes bigger than whales,

    aiming sticks that kill with fire, wielding long poles with a dying naked man
      whose bony toes they'll force you to kiss, he says,
but you must spit on his face, my brethren, throw dirt & scat, this god-man

who will enslave our people with dead promises of paradise, so resist these men
    with all your might. Burn down their huts, poison their water,
bewitch their canoes.

But if fire and magic fail then suicide is the holy of holies. With open eyes,
      hurl down from the highest cliffs & you'll live forever
in the birthing waters of our sea.

Minotaur

Isn't the bat birdier than a penguin, the whale fishier than an eel?
And doesn't the platypus lay eggs & the hammerhead shark bear
live young? There's no logic to creation. When a random sperm
wriggles into the wrong womb, monsters like me are made. I
am the impossible hybrid. The mule has nothing on me. Every
morning I ask myself, Should I be a man or an animal today? I
can compose dithyrambs to the dew of the moon, then just as fast
gore a man's skull like a mongongo nut. You men of reason call
me an abomination. *Confusion is in your blood*, you say. *Go live with
the beasts of the field & the anthropophagi & the cannibals too.* Watch
me crash through your labyrinths of caste. Watch me tear up your
cultivars of culture. I am the apostle of impurity, the inciter of
instinct, the confounder of nature. Hear me, my half-beast brothers,
my multitudes of the half-bred & the ill-bred. It is our destiny to
transgress biology. Let balance surrender to flux, let chaos overrun
God's handiwork. Join me in my crusade to break the curse of
wholeness, scatter rigid symmetries, untune all harmonies. Those
fractious fractions of our blood will be our legacy.

The Magnificent Jeremiah Expounds
on the Impending Doom of Miami

Tear your Gucci clothes, sprinkle dust on your Botox foreheads
& weep before the new diluvium comes to town—
Your precious Fisher Island, Coconut Grove, Key Biscayne,
Brickell, Coral Gables, etc., under miles of seawater,
High waves to smash bedrock easy as a malanga tuber.
This time no Noah & his ark to salvage the stragglers.
No milk and honey for you either, just salt upon salt,
Storm upon storm & your pleas to God will be bubbles
Of gas in an ear gone deafer than some woodworm or crab
& in one thousand years or the end of time if it comes before,
His angels of corrosion will have redeemed your wanton waste,
Your sins of effluent affluence & so returned every crevice
To rust, dust, gravel, sand, but in the meantime you will adapt
As the termite or the ant to any cataclysm & build hives
From God's debris of pickled wood, clammy gypsum,
Mashed limestone & you will catch fish with filed teeth,
Fingernails overgrown to claws & you will hold your breath
Longer than a dolphin or a seal, your spit turning to brine,
Your sweat ammoniac & your females will forgo birthing
To spawn in the caverns of rusting steel, stalactites of glass
Where you will learn to speak as whales beneath the fathoms
Of dark water & swim in pods of piety across the swells
As the new cetaceans of the Lord & when your skin glistens
With the slime of creation, your arms will flap to flippers,
Legs fuse to flukes & you will grow pinkish blowholes
That geyser the brine cherubs who sing to the end of days
& God will look upon you with his wide octopus eyes,
Happy that His seas have restored Eden's brood to purity.

Triptych Number 3: Víctor Manuel

I. Magdalena and the Mango Tree

riffing off Manuel's undated painting Landscape with Sunflowers

I am Magdalena with the owl eyes,
a long black braid like a horse's tail.
I wear a paper dress & coconut clogs
my mother made with spindly hands.
She is tall & skinny as a scarecrow
but can tell time better than any rooster.
She loves me more in dreams, she says,
and cannot cry unless an onion is in her eye.
Death will come soon enough, she says,
so go play before night claims her prey.
I hopscotch in the park of sunflowers
tall as royal palms & howl to the dogs
that take siestas in a kapok's shade.
A dozen widows in cobweb gowns
knit baby clothes from jumbles of yarn.
They shout in choral glee, *Sing us*
canticles to the papaya, lovely child,
sing us seguidillas to the chirimoya too.
I tell them no, no, you lady crows,
it's two o'clock, *merienda* time,
and my mother awaits with teas
of purslane & malanga fritters.
At our shrine of cowrie shells
we will pray to La Vírgen de Regla
with cups of seawater, lard lights,
and I will sign of the cross on
her lips, she the same to my eyes,
and before the last church bell rings

we will dance round our mango tree
with ripe fruit big as the kidneys of bulls
that graze in the graves of the stillborn,
those raggedy toddlers picked too soon,
and then at star-rise we will pig out
on the fallen stinky fruit with hands tied,
wet-earth knees, mouths bare, noses
rooting like the holy hogs of Bethlehem,
our slopped nostrils so deep, so deep
into skin, flesh & sap of everlasting life.

II. Manifesto

Before they bury me in a coffin of scrap wood with lead crumbs, I would like to paint on a canvas of sweet water with waves that go up and down like butterfly wings in a breeze of frankincense. I would look for my canvas in a river whose shores are the spongy womb of Mother Mary. Isn't water purer than soil since God created water first? Don't the unborn float joyfully in their warm amnions until the world wrenches them into a life of penuries and wants? With ferocious tone, your lips on fire, you ask me, Angel of Doubt, how would I paint on water since I'm an earthly creature, the son of mud and the grandson of slime? Whether I'm awake or asleep, you bring anguish into my world as if hope were just flotsam in some stagnant sea. You numb my hands when I take the brush. You make my eyes see blood when the sky is blue. You make me smell ammonia when I put a lily to my nose. You are wrong, so wrong. I will mock you as rust mocks steel, as termites mock wood, as rain mocks stone. I will find my own Eden on that river between mountains, my little boat safe and steady with its anchor of faith, and I will paint landscapes and still lifes with a brush big as an oar, my palette the rainbow, my light that of the sun that evaporates moans to Easter clouds.

III. Anaphora to a Small Cuban River

after Manuel's circa 1943 painting San Juan River, Matanzas

River of ruffles, more a creek or a runoff
than a proud & sovereign waterway,
a smudge of famished water on hard clay.

River of humped canoes & banana boats
urchin boys row in flotillas of carnaval
as nuns sleep siestas of guava marmalade.

River of red crabs whose claws are claves
that chatter canticles on Easter Sunday
when the poor get their alms of fatty *lechón*.

River of shallow houses with beaded doors
that welcome multitudes of the wayward,
the displaced, the haggard seeking charity.

River of redemption where cradles of corn husk
& vine bassinets wash into foundling houses
where the scrapped & cast-off bloom to wholeness.

River of memory that carves the stones
of sin into amulets of grace & makes us weep
our Taíno brethren burned for the Creed,
our African brethren shackled to sugar cane.

V

Balsero

after Luis Cruz Azaceta's 1992 screen print Fragile Crossing

Tell me, Our Lady, why must I see stars in the green billows,
twinkling to harbors safe as shrines, when it's just the gouged eyes
of angels blinking over sea hillocks with sulfurous peaks, crags that
spritz devil's spindrift, wavelets sharp as my machete that cut black
cane in Camagüey, a concentration camp on a bluff, condemned
three years for defaming the State. All I did was shout, *Fuck, Fidel!* in
a bread line. A horde scored my tongue, broke bones, jabbed needles
in the quicks of my nails. That first year I almost died of typhus, later
on pneumonia, afterward malaria. They call me Lazarus of the Sea. I
row against time, against the sidewinding waves, against the flotsam
of cyclones, my boat that crumples like cardboard, my oar a Cyclops'
toothpick, my tin compass from an old Cracker Jack box. Prayers
fade fast in the blue fog of twilight & I weep tears of bilge, moan the
shrapnel wind, touch the eyes of the Archangel Gabriel. *Don't waste
your breath*, he says. *God is deaf, mute & blind, might as well be dead.*
Grace is a castaway like me & Faith one more wreck on the seafloor.

El Patio de Mi Casa

after María Brito's 1990 mixed media of the same name

My patio was once a schoolyard, or maybe a barracoon, perhaps
both & the ghosts of children nest under the pink sink, mouths
agape for flakes of rust, or they creep to the ceiling, sucking on the
five taps of blue water, their little lips abuzz like cicadas. In the
moonlight I see them bounce on my feather bed, bowed like an old
donkey's back, or they teeter-totter in my wicker chair darned with
burlap string. Leave them alone, I say to my mother, who wants to
cleanse the house with carvacrol, trapping these children's souls in
beehives then stringing them up with kites so they fly to the moon.
Let them drum our dented pots, let them screech happy carols, let
them dance with tin spurs on their little feet. Mother, I don't care if
they nibble our family photos, soil your heirlooms of lace, or steal
what few grains of rice (more like gypsum ants) you hoard in the
pink pantry. Let them play cat's cradle with spiderwebs, let them
rummage in your armoire of moths, let them lurk in your shadows
of ill-will & tease you to laughter. Ghosts are unruly, free to be
fickle, unlike me, the pig-tailed girl you kept me strapped to the
sewing machine in the shed of planks by the mango tree too old
to fruit. Work & sweat will set you free, you said, just like Fidel on
the radio. Cut me out of those sepia photos on the wall, burn those
baby braids you keep in porcelain, toss my first-communion gown
into the sea. I wish I'd been born into a litter of mice, quick to grow,
quick to breed, quick to die among the kapok trees.

Lorca in the Forest of Goatskin Trees

At summer's equinox sunrays curdle to soursop,
calabash clouds drift on ginger currents to Africa,
and where the mountains shadow a blue-black sea,
the poet saunters alone through the forest

of goatskin trees sacred to the children of Ochá,
Cuba's first Yoruba, bozal slaves who breathed brine
on those Spanish brigs ballasted by their grief,
each plank sinew bound, nailed with teeth, bone, cochlea.

Lorca smells sweat of maroons in the leaves,
strokes roots that coil his wrist like newborn boas,
and as emery winds rustle the star-apple canopy,
his heart trembles to murmurous maracas;

that obsidian mane musses to green moss,
while his shorter leg, cause of his swaying gait,
grows without pain or shame to hardwood—
pith and phlegm of Ibadan, Oyo, Enugu.

Something falls from the spirit tree, not fruit
or seed but a fetish of coral and stone
with tiny crania set into eggshell cavities,
blue ribbons like entrails of lapis lazuli.

The fetish speaks to Lorca in Lucumí,
its consonants like rain pelting a lead river,
nasals that blare auroras, an arc of syllables
strung like the beaded sighs of *cante jondo*.

The poet presses the fetish to his belly
like tender parchment strained to elegy
then hears a song that gnaws the burls
and whorls of ears blessed to wild wood.

He learns the orisha's name, Eshu Elegba,
crossroader, soothsayer, gossip, trickster
of tricksters, loud and proud, no little duende
hiding way in the mouse holes of Granada.

And Lorca is no more a man but the drum
called Dundun—wood talker, skin whisperer—
whose voice rumbles hymnals of heartwood
across the hammock and up to the cloud forest,

where his song vibrates gourds to hatch
as hummingbirds that feed on blood orchids,
and the stillborn *chichereku* grow bat wings,
chirping congas in caverns of bromeliad.

Homage to Alejo Carpentier

On this Columbus Day, one thousand miles
from where his caravels cast anchors of greed & soon plowed
our Edenic islands to sugar's Babylon, I sing to you,
Don Alejo, who redeemed our islands' history
with a pen dipped in myths so often maligned & misaligned
by colonial bigotry. When Europe's hordes
were goose-stepping to the kettledrums of blood war,
you heard the animist songs of Mother Africa
so stubbornly alive in the creoles & the pidgins of the folk
who survived the cane fields & the barracoons.
Praise you, our master fabulist *de lo real maravilloso*,
who dreamt Castilian altars altered by the *batá* drums,
the smoke of *marabú*, the palm-fat candles
of Acrá that burn to gold at dusk when the baobab bats
take to the sienna skies of Damballah Weddo.

When you set sail from France to escape the Nazis
& visited Haiti for the first time, the duendes of vodun
touched your mouth as Yahweh did to Isaiah
& revealed that wild trees are spirits of bark & phloem,
that Mawoo is the moon that mounts the sun
to birth the stars, that the salt rains of Our Lady Oyá
can heal the penuries of a European mind
sickened by old supremacies of blood purity—
this world of ours so stippled, dappled, freckled, splotched
with impurities that bless all things to hallowedness.

Prayer for Obatalá

Cristo africano, clan of Ilé-Ifé
Who crossed the Middle Passage
Muzzled and tied with *cadenas*,
Who labored in the Via Dolorosa
Of machete and flogged *novenas*
Then died crucified at thirty-three
In the cane fields of Baraguá

O harbinger of hurricanes, floods, tempests
Who heals paralytics, mutes, hunchbacks,
Sweetest diviner, jovial and garrulous
When fed dove eggs in sweet meringue
But tongue-tied at the slightest hint of salt,

O powerful Obatalá who rides
Our shaved heads in the moonlight Mass
Of lambskin drums, conch trumpets,
King of the Lucumí who died for our sins,
Son of Olofi who gave us first breath

Brujerías

I am shaman
    magus
       palero
          obeah man
            babalawo
          soothsayer
            curandero
               oungan

I dance a *guaguancó* with St. Jerome
    seduce St. Teresa with coconut flan
convert John the Baptist to *santería*
    turn water to rum in Galilee
swing Shangó's double ax over Yahweh's tabernacle
    break Moses's rod
teach Columbus to divine with cowries
    shit guava buds in Queen Isabella's soup
sing to Yemayá in Ephesus
    train golem and zombis to kill Klansmen
eat the jowl of the Orange Puto POTUS
    seed Gitmo with figs of cimarrones
pray for the hurricane that takes away the sins of the world

Nonce Sonnet for Rousseau

Why spray to death the poison oak that cracks
My mildewed fence or pull the crab grass
Thriving in the bald patches of my lawn?
Yardwork is fucked-up, the Sex Pistols sing.
Let anarchy reign: decay's a natural thing.
Praise rot-wood, leaf-mold, red rust, fungal spawn.
Implore the worm, the termite, and the mole.
O prophet Rosseau, talk to me of soul.
How free it is without law, caste, or creed.
I want to be savage and eat bark of trees,
Drink green water, crawl rocks to cut my knees.
Purge me of words, abstractions, the screed
Of reason, logic's bane. Bless me: I—beast—
Mammal runt, grunt enchanter, muck's priest.

The Incredible Gringa Called Giganta

*after a 1940's tourist poster of a giant American woman in a yellow bikini
standing over the island of Cuba*

Look upon me and despair, you wiggly little island of mojitos &
maracas. I am Giganta, the five-mile woman with atom-bomb
thumbs & feet big as battleships that can stomp you like a cucaracha
if you misbehave. I am the Colossus of Capitalism too, Gargantua
of Gluttony, or even Lady Liberty but with a bombshell figure that
puts Jayne Mansfield to shame. Behold this waspy waist that took
months of dieting on grapefruit, this gangbuster bustline that stops
traffic on Fifth Avenue. And what are you, *cubanita*, just ninety miles
away? You are that lapdog we keep on a short leash of loans, liens &
late fees. How well we cook your books, how well we lubricate with
bribes. Now we are flush with cash & tourism is our game. Those
smelly old convents are gone & in their place casinos for the beehive
blondes to play baccarat & lose their nest eggs. Your beaches are
prime real estate where our hotels luxuriate on the finest sands in the
world & your warm sun revives our bodies so many months locked
in the coolers of our north. How we tan to a coppery sheen, a pure
metal to the gods, unlike your vulgar caramel. My loveliest señorita,
keep kowtowing to our business plan & you'll be a happy colony. Let
your rum fall like cataracts into our tongues, let your sassy bananas
mesmerize us with cha-cha-chas, let your roulette wheels spin us to
cyclones of desire.

Cuban Triolet

for Federico García Lorca

With sweet tobacco, black hens, dark rum
The sick & the broken pray to San Lazaró.
Cocks call, shrines glow, wheelchair girls come
With sweet tobacco, black hens, dark rum.
Crutches conga, slings sing, prostheses drum
For good health, more dollars, the death of woe.
With sweet tobacco, black hens, dark rum
The sick & the broken pray to San Lazaró.

Solar de la Habana ,
(In Praise of the Washerwomen)

inspired by the 1964 film We Are the Music!

Once a mansion, now a tenement called *solar*,
so close to Havana bay that spindrift floats
like incense into iron windows and every night
a cloister of gulls jabbers devotions to the moon—
this sea-hallowed warren of washerwomen,
fishers' widows who sing ditties, sea chanteys
from Calabar; sleep in pirogues; grow aloes,
brine orchids that heal burns, blisters, and sprains;
hoist laundry to crosstrees of *ceiba pentandra*
that dries fast in the Antilles' smoldering dusk.
Day after day, by sunlight or moonlight,
they press vestments with charcoal irons,
stoke scrap-wood fires, stir heirloom cauldrons
where laundry boils to baptismal cleanness
to be scrubbed with wrinkled hands, high born,
until their sweat crystallizes to rosary beads.
Once the work is done they gather in the courtyard
by la Fuente, fountain of life, drawing holy water
in terracotta chalices for Our Lady of Regla,
the black Virgin, Ave María, la Madre Morena,
whose glass shrine sits on mangrove stilts
circled by white sand. They light bamboo lamps,
drum bongos, clack coconut castanets, singing hymns
that mix Latin with Yoruba, and the youngest
shouts out she's seen Our Lady dance *la rumba*
in gyres, shimmies, twists, and they all huddle
in throes of alleluia, blessed spasms, joyous
exaltations of washboard, lye soap, and hot iron.

Skin

in memory of the Cuban Poet Gabriel de la Concepción Valdés
(aka Plácido), 1809–1844

The tobacco flower so white and free of dusk,
yet its leaves so brown they eclipse the sun,
and you, my Placido, another contradiction,
an octoroon orphaned at birth, so light the nuns
thought you white till your hair began to kink,
then the abbess's pen decreed you colored,
and you would learn to walk fast in shadows,
doff your hat at all white men, poor or rich,
murmuring "your mercy" with eyes downcast.

Poeta mulato, they called you, more brass
than bronze but never *trigueño*, the color
of young wheat, reserved for Spanish blood.
By day you made hair combs of tortoise shell,
so popular with the ladies who wear mantillas
and twirl their fans in lacquered carriages,
then by candlelight you taught yourself to craft
ottava rimas with borrowed books, bartered ink,
all kinds of encomia too for the planter class
you'd recite for a few coins at the governor's balls.

The girl you loved, a *veguera*, tobacco grower,
Canarian stock, was tanned to oak or cinnamon,
yet still a *trigueña* and by Spanish law white,
so marriage impossible, friendship suspicious.
"Why can I not be wheat or vanilla," you plead
to God. "Isn't that my birthright, so close

to being white the angels cannot tell me apart?
Inside me night does not exist, all darkness
dies to light, my mind's whiteness so clean
it is a moon reborn when the cyclone season is gone."

The law is adamant, so says God through the priest,
the lawyer, the soldier: It is not skin skin
but soul soul that makes whiteness white,
and black can never transmute to perfection.
What Africa tinges remains tinged for eternity.
Black skin is thick as hide, impermeable, obdurate
with sin, and can never admit the light of God,
unlike white skin so thin, gossamer—moth-winged—
that it crackles like an angel's under moonlight.

Triptych Number 4: Wifredo Lam

I. Mythopoesis

inspired by Lam's 1947 painting Character with Two Elegguas

You are not a monster that haunts the mind
                        as in Goya's aquatint but the child
of Ogún, blacksmith's orisha. You are Irin Obirin, metallic Eve
born of African ore wombed in the forge
                           of Caná-Caná,
                  iron vulture that glides between heaven's
             molten seas & this carboniferous earth
where your twin sprites
        —iron Elegguas—
              breathe the rust of creation
inside your ferruginous baobabs. How happy
                       they are to perch by day
on your bladed shoulders whistling gunmetal carols,
                            blowing bubbles of brass.

Or when they are bored & mischievous
they roll in the wet clods of black clay along the banks of alkaline rivers
                  across swamplands of dross & slag.

You are the harbinger of the hybrid, mother of the mongrel,
                holiest mulata of metal & wood & all things
                opposite in kind, in spirit & in blood.

You alone can make wood & metal fuse into a harmonious whole,
                       this blessed chimera
sprung from flux, blast, scum, knot, knurl, etc.,
                    so glaring, so glorious.

But I am a vagrant human, uncoupled, unbetrothed, unrooted.
                                    I wish I had a wooden body
with metal hands to touch you in glee, perhaps a little cocky too,

but all I do is tremble with fear
seeing your face smelted & hammered down to a mare
                            of war: armored teeth & furnace nostrils.

Mother Eve, why does your anvil forehead
feel so hot on my fingertips that I must douse them
in a barrel of water? And when I caress your beard of wire-tasseled buttocks

(or are they cannonballs?) every hair in my body
pricks up like the iron tacks of a martyr

& I begin to fantasize about being one of those armored fish
from Devonian times with hardwood bones,
scales of chainmail, acorn eyes, a mouth like toothy pliers

                        & you will then call me your love child
                        with the spiky hair, the clacking bones

& you will sing me lullabies of fire & smoke,
cradle me in your cauldron's belly,

                    nurse me with your spigot breasts until that last breath

when all living things must corrode to the eternal swarf & sawdust.

II. Manifesto

From the orishas I learned to paint trees in human form, excess of
buttocks and breasts, excess of sap that bursts from caesarian clefts
and flows into our sea of ghosts where the angels are giant hermit
crabs that dispose of the scaly dead with forged claws and teeth of
assegai. My strangler figs are those maroons my godmother invoked
at moonrise, feral and free in their palisades of flesh and bone where
big-bellied drums beat out songs of rebellion heard from Baracoa to
Matahambre. Our jungle is a labyrinth of caustic colors, tenebrous
hues, jagged lines that lash the horizon, except when the setting sun's
linseed light softens them to a childlike grace. This is my canvas,
where dark pigments bless newborn skin and the brush follows the
trails of blood from village to barracoon. This is my frame of black
snakes, Vodun Danballahs, that protect my art from jealous eyes
and racist tongues. This is my garden of frets and arrows, where the
orishas can live out their days in cauldrons of honeyed pitch and
cowrie shells.

III. Cosmology

colloquy with Lam's 1942 oil-on-paper painting Venus or Nude in White

In between incantations and sips of *café cubano*, you tell me that
    Boticelli's Venus
is a lie, a false idealization of scales and sea-foam, a woman whose
    creamy whiteness
would curdle to goat cheese in our tropical light, this muse stealthier
    than the salt
that wrinkles ebony skin, a perverse idolatry with hair like filaments
    of gold,
which should, if God is just, be crinkles of black coral or the inky
    ripples of a cuttlefish.
Your Venus, you argue, is Yemayá Olokún, orisha of darkest waters,
    Our Lady
with the head of a sawfish and lips of crimson sea cucumber: Behold
    those thick,
powerful lips, you command—*ay bemba colorá, ay bemba sagraá*—that
    open and close
her grottoed mouth, where stingrays breed cherubim and the vipers of
    night molt mercury.
I am a warrior artist, you exclaim in spindrift shouts, your weapons
    those brushes,
pencils, charcoal sticks you use to fight the racists who swear that
    beauty is pure white
but never that purest blackness in the mind of Father Olodumare,
    who dreamed
the black holes before they had a name, who dwelled in nothingness,
    the bliss
of zero, without the greed of matter, before the curse of time, before
    that upstart Jehova
and his cataclysm of light exiled Olodumare and made white the
    tyrant of black.

Acknowledgments

I am grateful to those journals where these poems first appeared, sometimes in earlier forms and with different titles.

African-American Review: "Homage to Alejo Carpentier," "Skin," and "Cuban Triolet"

Boulevard: "St. Apollonia, Patroness of Dentists"

Chiricú Journal: Latina/o Literatures, Arts, and Cultures: "Triptych Number 1: Fidelio Ponce"

The Cincinnati Review: "The Blackberry Tree"

Colorado Review: "St. Tatua, Patroness of Tattooists"

Hayden's Ferry Review: "Brujerías"

Hotel Amerika: "St. Lucy, Patroness of Those Troubled by Their Eyes," "The Transverberation of St. Teresa of Ávila," "St. Teresa of Ávila upon Reading the *Song of Songs*," and "Caliban to the Sea Nymph Ananai"

The Hudson Review: "Mercato del Pesce, Catania," "Hüzün," "Off-Off-Variation on Théophile Gautier's 'Promenade Nocturne,'" and Part III ("Cosmology") of "Triptych Number 4: Wifredo Lam"

Literary Matters [literarymatters.org]: "First Communion," "Triptych Number 3: Víctor Manuel," "The Magnificent Jeremiah Expounds on the Impending Doom of Miami," "Letter to José Lezama Lima," and "Minotaur"

MiPOesias: "Sister Aurea, OCD, Rails against the Animals to Her Third Graders"

Pilgrimage: "Prayer for Obatalá"

Poetry Magazine: "El Patio de Mi Casa," "Altar Boy," and "Hear Me, Hart Crane"

Prairie Schooner: "Balsero," "Solar de la Habana (In Praise of the Washerwomen)," and "Lorca in the Forest of Goatskin Trees"

Presence: A Journal of Catholic Poetry: "Ode" and "Ezan"

The Yale Review: "Triptych Number 2: Carlos Enríquez"

"Tower of Babel" appeared as a "Poem-a-Day" on November 2, 2021, at the website of the Academy of American Poets, https://www.poets.org.

"St. Lapsia, Patroness for Catholics Lapsed & Re-Lapsed" and "Turuqueira" appeared in the online anthology *A Given Grace: An Anthology of Christian Poems*, edited by Desmond Kon and Eric Valles (Squircle Line Press, 2021), http://www.squirclelinepress.org.

"Grace" appeared May 20, 2019, as a "Poem-of-the-Week" on the *Missouri Review* website, https://www.missourireview.com.